How Can Jane Help?

by Lili Henderson
illustrated by Katie McDee

"Can I help?" said Jane.

"Help clean the cage," said Gabe.

"Can I help?" said Jane.

"Help clean the car,"
said Grace.

"Can I help?" said Jane.

"Help make lunch,"
said Mom.

"Can I help?" said Jane.

"Help with the bags," said Dad.

"Can I help?" said Jane.

"Help me rake," said
Mrs. Long.

"Now how can I help?"
said Jane.

"I can help you, too,"
she said.